10/98

West Africa

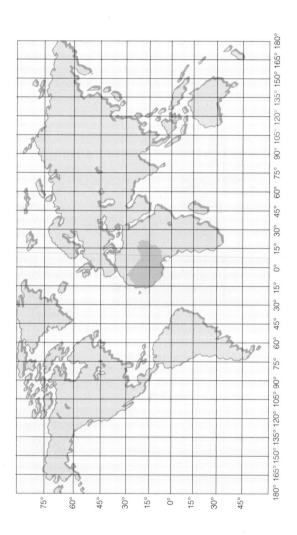

180° 165° 150° 135° 120° 105° 90° 75° 60° 45° 30° 15° 0° 15° 30° 45° 60° 75° 90° 105° 120° 135° 150° 165° 180°

75°
60°
45°
30°
15°
0°
15°
30°
45°

WEST AFRICA

Country	country area (sq mi)	population (1995)	capital	currency
BENIN	43,485	5,400,000	Porto Novo	CFA Franc (CFAF) = 100 centimes
BURKINA FASO	105,875	10,300,000	Ouagadougou	CFA Franc (CFAF) = 100 centimes
CAPE VERDE	1,555	372,000	Praia	1 Cape Verde Escudo (CVEsc) = 100 centavos
CÔTE D'IVOIRE	124,510	14,300,000	Yamoussoukro	CFA Franc (CFAF) = 100 centimes
THE GAMBIA	4,360	1,100,000	Banjul	Dalasi (D) = 100 Bututs
GHANA	92,110	17,500,000	Accra	New Cedi (C) = 100 pesewas
GUINEA	94,930	6,700,000	Conakry	Guinea Franc (FG) = 100 centimes
GUINEA-BISSAU	13,950	1,100,000	Bissau	CFA Franc (CFAF) = 100 centimes
LIBERIA	43,000	3,000,000	Monrovia	Liberian Dollar (L$) = 100 cents
MALI	478,800	10,800,000	Bamako	CFA Franc (CFAF) = 100 centimes
MAURITANIA	397,980	2,300,000	Nouakchott	Ouguiya (UM) = 5 Khoums
NIGER	489,230	9,200,000	Niamey	CFA Franc (CFAF) = 100 centimes
NIGERIA	356,700	111,700,000	Abuja	Naira (N) = 100 Kobo
SENEGAL	75,750	8,300,000	Dakar	CFA Franc (CFAF) = 100 centimes
SIERRA LEONE	27,700	4,500,000	Freetown	Leone (Le) = 100 cents
TOGO	21,930	4,100,000	Lomé	CFA Franc (CFAF) = 100 centimes

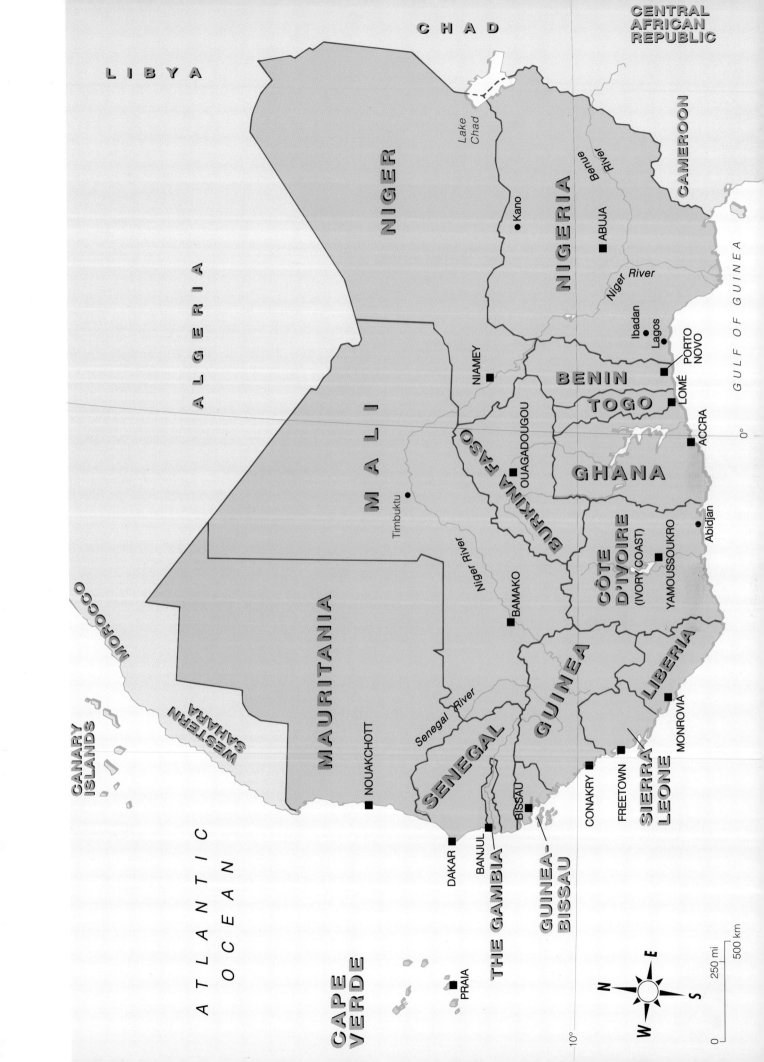

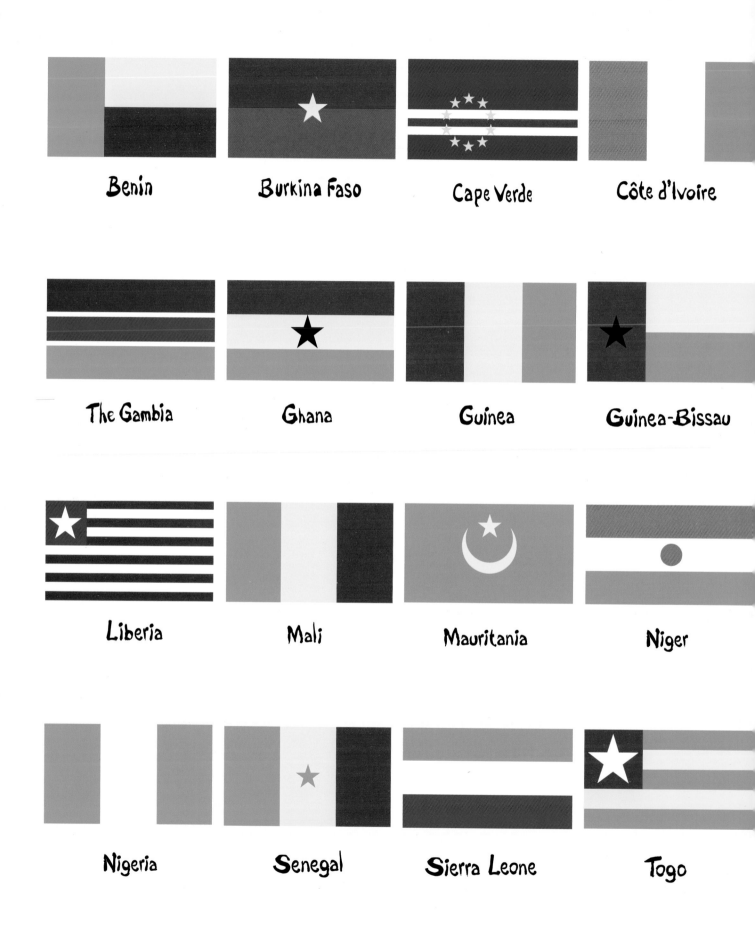

Benin

Burkina Faso

Cape Verde

Côte d'Ivoire

The Gambia

Ghana

Guinea

Guinea-Bissau

Liberia

Mali

Mauritania

Niger

Nigeria

Senegal

Sierra Leone

Togo

West Africa

Tony Binns and Rob Bowden

RSVP
RAINTREE
Steck-Vaughn
PUBLISHERS
The Steck-Vaughn Company

Austin, Texas

Published by Raintree Steck-Vaughn Publishers, an imprint of Steck-Vaughn Company

Design and typesetting Roger Kohn Designs
Commissioning editor Hazel Songhurst
Editor Merle Thompson
Assistant editor Diana Russell
Picture research Paula Chapman
Maps János Márffy

We are grateful to the following for permission to reproduce photographs:
Front Cover: Panos *above*;
Axiom (James Morris) *below*
Axiom, pages 12 *below*, (James Morris), 18 (James Morris), 35 (James Morris), 37 (James Morris), 45 (James Morris); Tony Binns, pages 34 *above*, 40, 42 left; Colorific, page 36 (Carl Purcell); Eye Ubiquitous, pages 11 *above* (Thelma Sanders), 16 (Mark Newham), 17 (A. Hibbert); FLPA, page 41 (E & D Hosking); Getty Images, page 8 *below* (Steven Rothfield); Robert Harding, page 12 *above*, 13, 19 *below*, 43; Impact, pages 9 (Caroline Penn), 10 *above* (Carolyn Bates), 19 *above* (David Palmer), 22 (Caroline Penn), 23 *above* (Caroline Penn), 32 (Caroline Penn), 33 (Caroline Penn), 42 *right* (David Palmer); Link, page 24 *above and below* (Ron Giling); Panos, pages 14 (J. Hartley), 20 (Bruce Paton), 25 (Betty Press), 27 (Liba Taylor), 28 *right* (Betty Press), 29 (Jon Spaull), 30 (Jeremy Hartley), 31 (Ron Giling), 34 *below* (Ron Giling), 38 *above* (Liba Taylor), 38 *below* (Jeremy Hartley), 39 (Ian Cartwright), 44 (Betty Press); John Spaull, pages, 10/11 *below*; Still Pictures, page 15 (Martin Wright); Topham, pages 26, 28 *left*; Werner Foreman, page 8 *above*; WPL, page 21, 23 *below*.

The statistics given in this book are the most up-to-date available at the time of going to press.

Printed in Hong Kong by Wing King Tong

Library of Congress Cataloging-in-Publication Data
Binns, Tony.
    West Africa / Tony Binns and Rob Bowden.
        p.   cm. — (Country fact files)
    Includes bibliographical references and index.
    Summary: Introduces the landscape, climate, natural resources, people, and culture of the countries of West Africa.
        ISBN 0-8172-5400-5 (alk. paper)
    1. Africa, West — Juvenile literature. [1. Africa, West.]
        I. Bowden, Rob. II. Title. III. Series.
                DT471.B39   1998
    966 — dc21   97-40252
                                            CIP   AC

1 2 3 4 5 6 7 8 9 0 HK 01 00 99 98 97

CONTENTS

Words that are explained in the glossary are printed in
SMALL CAPITALS the first time they are mentioned in the text.

INTRODUCTION

For the purpose of this book, West Africa is defined as the 16 countries that belong to the Economic Community of the West African States (ECOWAS). These are: Benin, Burkina Faso, Cape Verde, Côte d'Ivoire (Ivory Coast), Ghana, Guinea, Guinea-Bissau, Liberia, Mali, Mauritania, Niger, Nigeria, Senegal, Sierra Leone, The Gambia, and Togo. All are countries on the African mainland with the exception of Cape Verde, a group of islands in the Atlantic Ocean off the west coast of Mauritania and Senegal.

West Africa contains dense forests, vast expanses of desert and grassland, environmentally important wetland areas, and many large, sprawling cities.

◀ *A 16th-century brass head of Idia, the Queen Mother of the Benin Kingdom in southern Nigeria. The Benin Kingdom is famous for metalworking.*

▼ *A Dogon village clinging to the lower slopes of the Bandiagara Escarpment in Mali. Such densely settled villages stand between the plateau above, where intensive vegetable cultivation is practiced, and the millet and sorghum fields on the plains below.*

▲ **This is a scene from rush hour in Cotonou, Benin. West Africa has many large cities that are growing very quickly.**

- Total area: 2,367,510 square miles (6,131,390 square km)
- Total population (1995): 210.7 million
- Population density (1995): Average of 88 people per square mile (313 per square mile in Nigeria; 5 per square mile in Mauritania)
- Largest cities (by population): Lagos 4,100,000; Abidjan 2,200,000; Dakar 1,730,000; Ibadan 2,000,000; Conakry 810,000; Bamako 746,000
- Longest river: Niger, 2,600 miles (4,180 km)
- Largest lake: Lake Chad, 10,040 square miles (26,000 square km)
- Major resources: Oil, timber, bauxite, uranium, rutile (titanium dioxide)
- Major products: Cocoa, coffee, cotton
- Environmental problems: Soil erosion, DESERTIFICATION, water shortages

The region has a long and rich cultural history. During the Middle Ages, West Africa already had long-established trade routes across the great Sahara Desert. Trading centers along the desert's southern edge, such as Kano, Timbuktu, Djenne, and Mopti, thrived. Metal bars and cowrie shells were used as currency. A number of powerful states controlled parts of the SAVANNA and semiarid regions and, farther south in the forest, kingdoms known for sophisticated mining and metalworking existed in Ashanti and Benin.

From the 16th to the 19th centuries, West Africa supplied millions of slaves to the Caribbean or to many of the southern states in the U.S. to work on plantations. They were gathered together in forts along the coast before being transferred there by ship. Many died during the journey because of the poor conditions on the ships. Starting in the mid-19th century, West Africa was gradually divided among the European powers.

A period of about 80 years of COLONIALISM followed, during which education, health, and legal systems were introduced. Vast quantities of mineral resources and CASH CROPS were sent to Europe during this time.

Today, more than 30 years after most countries have gained their INDEPENDENCE, West Africa is one of the poorest regions in the world. Living standards are often extremely low, and unstable political and economic conditions have prevented any improvement in the lives of most people. But it is a fascinating region nevertheless, with great potential, and this book explores its people, environments, and future prospects.

THE LANDSCAPE

One of the most impressive attributes of the West African region is its varied landscape. Moving northward from the Nigerian coast, the landscape changes from the mangroves of the Niger DELTA, to the tropical forests of southern Nigeria, the savanna bushland around Abuja, and the savanna grassland around the northern city of Kano. Crossing into Niger, the conditions become increasingly ARID as you move into a landscape known as the Sahel. This is an Arabic word meaning the "shore." In this case the shore is that of the great Sahara Desert. These distinct environmental zones, roughly parallel to the coast, are characteristic of most of West Africa.

The 16 West African countries vary greatly in size, ranging from tiny Cape Verde (1,555 square miles/4,030 sq km) to the

◀ **The Bandiagara Escarpment in Dogon country, southeast Mali, is over 93 miles (150 km) long and is a major upland feature in this part of West Africa.**

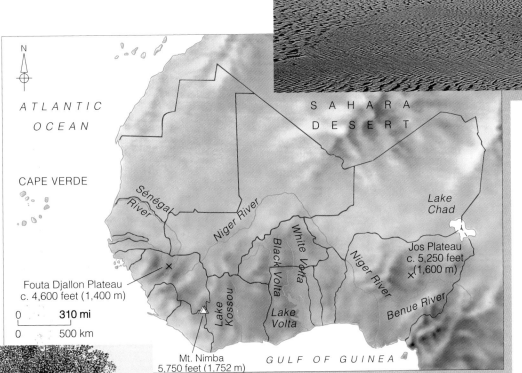

N

ATLANTIC
OCEAN

CAPE VERDE

SAHARA
DESERT

Sénégal River

Niger River

Black Volta

White Volta

Lake Kossou

Lake Volta

Niger River

Lake Chad

Jos Plateau
c. 5,250 feet
(1,600 m)

Benue River

Fouta Djallon Plateau
c. 4,600 feet (1,400 m)

0   310 mi
0   500 km

Mt. Nimba
5,750 feet (1,752 m)

GULF OF GUINEA

▲ **The Sahara Desert covers large parts of northern West Africa. This is a typical scene of sand dunes and a desert oasis in Mauritania. Other areas of the desert are much stonier than this.**

◀ **This is one of the mangrove swamps in Sierra Leone. The dense mangrove vegetation thrives in the salty water of the creeks and estuaries of rivers. Mangroves grow on stilt roots to keep their leaves above the high-tide level.**

vast desert state of Niger (489,230 square miles/1,267,000 sq km). Burkina Faso, Mali, and Niger are the only LANDLOCKED states in West Africa. The rest share the Atlantic coastline. The shapes of several of the states are unusual because their boundaries were drawn by European colonial powers in the Treaty of Berlin in 1885. Mali, for example, has straight borders with Mauritania and Algeria, while Togo and Benin are long and narrow.

Most of West Africa consists of plains and basins that rarely exceed 1,640 feet (500 m) above sea level. However, there are a few significant upland areas, such as the Fouta Djallon Plateau in Guinea, the Jos and

◄ *The Niger River is an important source of fish, as well as water for irrigation. It also acts as a transportation route to inland areas such as Niger.*

Mambila plateaus in Nigeria, and the Freetown Peninsula in Sierra Leone. These range between 2,625 and 4,920 feet (800 and 1,500 m). Rising above all of these are mountain peaks, such as Bintumani (6,391 feet/1,948 m) in Sierra Leone and Dimlang (6,693 feet/2,040 m) on the Nigeria–Cameroon border.

West Africa's major river is the Niger River. With a length of 2,597 feet (4,180 km), it is the third longest river in Africa. It rises in the Fouta Djallon Plateau of Guinea in the west, flows northward through Mali to Timbuktu, then bends sharply south through Niger and into Nigeria. It is joined there from the east by the Benue River (851 miles/1,370 km) about 310 miles (500 km) from the coast. The Niger is unusual in having two deltas— the so-called "inland delta" of Mali, and the coastal delta in Nigeria. The inland delta is one of the major wetlands of Africa. Irrigated rice and cotton are grown there, and fish are caught locally. Other major rivers in the region are the Senegal (1,000 miles/1,610 km), the Volta (900 miles/1,448 km), and the Gambia (700 miles/1,125 km).

The two largest lakes in West Africa are Lake Chad, bordering Nigeria and Niger,

▲ *Rain forest once covered much of the southern parts of West Africa, but most of it was destroyed for farming or timber extraction. Here, some of the rain forest in Cross River State, Nigeria, has regenerated after a period of cultivation.*

KEY FACTS

● The largest mainland country in West Africa, Niger, is 112 times bigger than Gambia, which is the smallest.

● With an area of 39,770 square miles (103,000 sq km), the inland Niger Delta in Mali is almost as big as the combined areas of Belgium, the Netherlands, and Switzerland.

● Lake Volta stretches over 250 miles (400 km) from the Akosombo Dam into the northern savanna interior of Ghana, providing fishing and water for irrigating crops.

● The Niger Delta in Nigeria is the largest in Africa, covering an area of 14,015 square miles (36,300 sq km) and with a coastline of almost 118 miles (190 km).

● In the 15th century, Portuguese sailors thought the mountains of the Freetown peninsula resembled a sleeping lion. They called them "Serra Lyoa," meaning "lion mountains." The name that was later chosen for the country was Sierra Leone.

and Lake Volta in Ghana. Lake Chad covers an area of 10,040 square miles (26,000 sq km). Lake Volta (3,280 square miles/8,500 sq km) was created in 1966 when the Akosombo Dam was built across the Volta River to generate HYDROELECTRICITY.

The West African coastline stretches for 3,170 miles (5,100 km) and dips gently into the sea. There are many sandbars and LAGOONS, but few harbors suitable for large ships. Freetown is a rare example of a natural deepwater harbor. The other major ports in West Africa, such as Lagos and Abidjan, developed only after large-scale construction work. Lagos is reached through a lagoon that requires regular dredging, and the Vridi Canal had to be cut through a sandbar to allow access to Abidjan.

▼ *A beach outside Lomé, in Togo. West Africa's coastline has many wide, sandy beaches with great potential for tourism. Many beaches are fringed with coconut palms. The shells of the coconuts are often used as fuel in neighboring towns and cities.*

◀ The Harmattan is a major feature of the West African climate. Localized dust storms, such as this one in Burkina Faso, are common prior to the arrival of the rains.

Rainfall is the key factor in shaping West Africa's different environmental zones. As a general rule, inland from the coast the climate becomes drier, but some upland areas have higher rainfall and lower temperatures than the surrounding lowlands. On the coast the region has a single distinct rainy season between May and October, but at the edge of the Sahara Desert, the rainy season is shorter (June/July to August/September) and much less reliable. Timbuktu, for example, receives just over 7.8 inches (200 mm) of rain annually.

TYPES OF VEGETATION

N

0   310 mi
   500 km

- Rain forest
- Mountain vegetation
- Thorn woodland and semidesert vegetation
- Broad-leaved woodland and wooded grassland
- Desert

KEY FACTS

● Freetown's annual rainfall (135 inches/3,434 mm) is almost four times that of Manchester, U.K. (34 inches/859 mm) and more than three times that of New York (43 inches/1,092 mm).

● Parts of Nigeria and Sierra Leone may experience over 210 thunderstorms per year, and the largest storms may last over eight hours.

● In colonial times West Africa was known as "The White Man's Grave" due to the disease, heat, and humidity. The cool Harmattan wind, which was sometimes called "The African Doctor," provided the only relief.

● The savanna and the Sahel regions had major droughts in the 1910s, 1940s, and 1970s. The rains were below average every year between 1970 and 1990.

Almost all of this falls in the months from June to September.

Parts of the West African coast, by contrast, receive more rainfall than almost anywhere else in Africa. Freetown, the capital of Sierra Leone, has an annual rainfall of 135 inches (3,434 mm) compared with 37.7 inches (958 mm) in Nairobi, (Kenya), and 20 inches (508 mm) in Cape Town (South Africa). Most of Freetown's rain falls between April and November, and with temperatures approaching 86°F (30°C), humidity is extremely high. The beginning and end of the rainy season are characterized by spectacular storms, often with strong winds, thunder, and lightning.

Temperatures across West Africa are high throughout the year; the average monthly temperature never falls below 64°F (18°C). In general the temperature range is lowest near the coast and increases as you move inland. The greatest ranges in temperature occur during the Harmattan Period, when daytime temperatures may be over 104°F (40°C) and can then drop below 43°F (6°C) at night in inland areas. The Harmattan is a dry, dusty wind, bringing cool air from the Sahara Desert between December and March. It can even reach the coast for short periods. The dust can be so thick that cars need to use their headlights in the middle of the day. People often suffer from cracked skin and colds.

◀ *Thunderstorms with torrential rain are typical at the beginning of the rainy season. They can cause flash floods that make some roads impassable.*

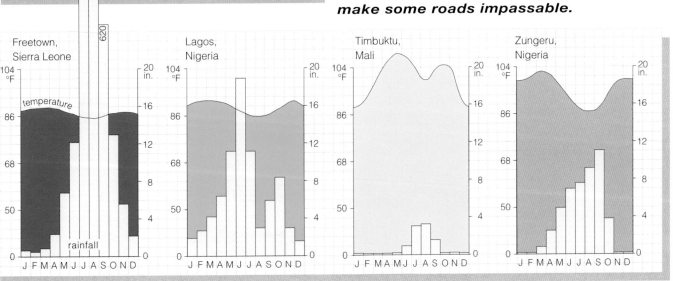

NATURAL RESOURCES

West Africa is rich in mineral resources. There are oil, coal, and tin in Nigeria, bauxite in Guinea, gold in Ghana, diamonds and rutile in Sierra Leone, iron ore in Mauritania, and uranium in Niger. Many of these resources are found only in remote areas, making them difficult or expensive to extract, and any POLITICAL INSTABILITY in the region can further complicate production. Some minerals are particularly abundant. For example, Guinea is the world's second largest producer of bauxite (which is used in the production of aluminum), and Niger is the second largest producer of uranium, Canada being the first.

Nigeria is Africa's largest producer of oil, which was first extracted from wells in the Niger Delta in the late 1950s. Production increased significantly in the early 1970s, and since 1973, oil has accounted for over 90 percent of Nigeria's total export earnings.

Some 70 to 80% of West Africans still rely on wood for fuel, and in rural areas wood is often the only available source of energy. In urban areas, electricity generated from hydroelectric power plants, such as Akosombo Dam in Ghana, supplies the needs of industry and wealthier households. But even in large cities, many of the poorer people must rely on wood brought in from surrounding rural areas. Timber is also exported, and West Africa accounts for 6.4% of world production, with Nigeria alone accounting for 3.5% in 1993. In the 1970s natural rubber was produced in Liberia, and a vast plantation was owned by

▼ *The Akosombo Dam in Ghana, which is situated at the southern end of Lake Volta. Hydroelectric power is an important source of electricity in some West African countries.*

► *Bark is stripped from hardwood tree trunks at Abidjan Harbor, Côte d'Ivoire. Timber production is important to local economies, but if left uncontrolled it can lead to severe environmental damage.*

KEY FACTS

● In 1970 Sierra Leone produced 2,050,000 carats of diamonds. In 1993 production fell to 350,000 carats.

● In 1994 Ghana, formerly Gold Coast, was the world's ninth largest producer of gold. In precolonial times, the Ashanti region in southwestern Ghana, with its capital Kumasi, was referred to as "the Kingdom of Gold."

● In 1970 Guinea produced 2.6 million tons of bauxite; in 1994 this figure had increased by more than 500% to 13.8 million tons.

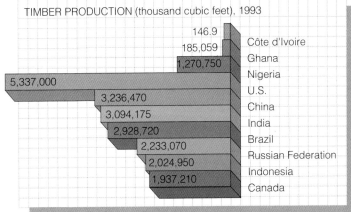

TIMBER PRODUCTION (thousand cubic feet), 1993

146.9	Côte d'Ivoire
185,059	Ghana
1,270,750	Nigeria
5,337,000	U.S.
3,236,470	China
3,094,175	India
2,928,720	Brazil
2,233,070	Russian Federation
2,024,950	Indonesia
1,937,210	Canada

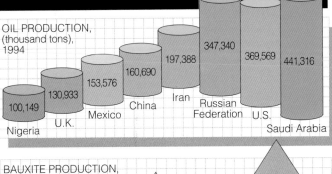

OIL PRODUCTION, (thousand tons), 1994

100,149	Nigeria
130,933	U.K.
153,576	Mexico
160,690	China
197,388	Iran
347,340	Russian Federation
369,569	U.S.
441,316	Saudi Arabia

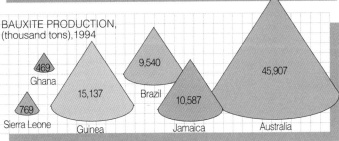

BAUXITE PRODUCTION, (thousand tons), 1994

469	Ghana
769	Sierra Leone
15,137	Guinea
9,540	Brazil
10,587	Jamaica
45,907	Australia

the Firestone Company. Liberia's recent civil war and continuing political unrest have slowed production.

The land remains the basic resource for most people and is used to grow food crops such as rice, corn, millet, yams, and cassava. It also provides important cash crops such as cocoa, coffee, cotton, and peanuts. The importance of land as a resource is reflected in the fact that so many of the region's major exports are agricultural commodities.

In 1995 the total population of West Africa was just over 210 million. This population is unevenly distributed, with 53 percent of people living in just one country, Nigeria, which covers only 15 percent of the region's total land area. With 111.7 million people, Nigeria has more people than any other African country. Its closest rivals are Egypt,

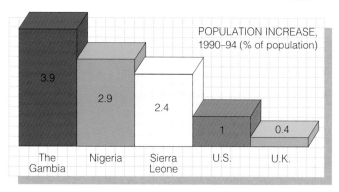

POPULATION INCREASE, 1990–94 (% of population)

The Gambia	Nigeria	Sierra Leone	U.S.	U.K.
3.9	2.9	2.4	1	0.4

▲ *West Africa has a wealth of traditional cultures. These musicians in Nigeria are helping to preserve such traditions from one generation to another.*

with 62.9 million, and Ethiopia, with 55.1 million. In sharp contrast, Cape Verde has only 372,000 people, and both The Gambia and Guinea-Bissau each have 1.1 million. Even large countries like Niger and Mauritania have relatively small populations, with 9.2 million and 2.3 million, respectively. Nigeria has 47 people per square mile, whereas Niger has 3 and Mauritania less than one. For further comparison, the U.K. has a population density of 94 people per square mile, and the U.S. has 75.

The ancient city of Kano, in northern Nigeria, is densely populated. It includes a number of pits from which building materials have been excavated. The pits are now filled with water and have become a serious health hazard. They are a breeding ground for mosquitoes and other pests.

Population growth rates in West Africa are among the highest in the world, exceeded only by Middle Eastern states such as Jordan and Yemen. The Gambia had an average annual growth rate of 3.9% between 1990 and 1994, and Côte d'Ivoire recorded 3.6% over the same period. Even Guinea-Bissau's growth rate of 2% is double the growth rate of the United States and five times that of the U.K.

URBANIZATION

Although the West African region is still predominantly rural, towns and cities are growing more rapidly than the general population. Burkina Faso, for example, almost doubled its average urban growth rate each year, from 5.5% between 1965

▶ *Lagos is West Africa's largest city, with about 4,100,000 inhabitants. Modern high-rise tower structures dominate the colonial buildings in the foreground. The harbor can be seen in the distance.*

◀ *It is common for people throughout West Africa to live in extended family groups. This family compound in Ghana is home to a man with several wives and many children.*

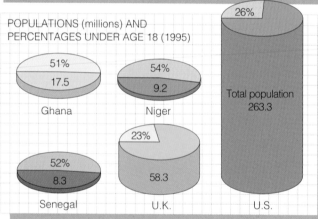

POPULATIONS (millions) AND
PERCENTAGES UNDER AGE 18 (1995)

51% / 17.5 — Ghana

54% / 9.2 — Niger

52% / 8.3 — Senegal

23% / 58.3 — U.K.

26% / Total population 263.3 — U.S.

A.D. 1000 and became an important religious and educational center, with the first university established in West Africa. Farther east, in what is now northern Nigeria, Kano had 75,000 inhabitants in the 16th century. In southwestern Nigeria, Ile-Ife, the

and 1980, to 10.4% between 1980 and 1995. One of the causes of this very rapid growth is the movement of people from rural areas, a process called RURAL-URBAN MIGRATION. The towns and cities cannot grow fast enough to cope with this migration, and people have started building their own homes out of basic materials on the outskirts of many large settlements. These shantytowns are often very crowded and without fresh water or proper sanitation.

Unlike other parts of Africa, many towns and cities in West Africa have a long history. Timbuktu, for example, was founded around

KEY FACTS

● Mauritania and Cape Verde are the most urbanized countries in the region. In 1992 about 50% of the population were living in towns and cities.
● In Nigeria alone no fewer than 395 different languages have been identified. In some cases a single language, such as Yoruba, may have many dialects.
● Elmina Castle was built on the Ghanaian coast by the Portuguese in the late 15th century. It is the oldest and largest of more than 20 fortifications built by the European powers to house slaves awaiting ships to take them across the Atlantic.

◀ *Men dressed in their best clothes sit and chat after attending Friday prayers at a mosque in northern Nigeria.*

spiritual capital of the Yoruba people, was established by the 10th century. Later many other large towns developed. Today Yorubaland is probably the most urbanized part of the African continent.

ETHNIC GROUPS AND LANGUAGES

West Africa is among the most diverse ethnic regions in the world. It is possible that more languages are spoken there than in any other region of similar size. Although French, English, and Portuguese were "official" languages during the colonial period, tribal languages have remained very strong. This is because, unlike other parts of Africa, there were few European settlers in the region. Arabic is widely spoken throughout West Africa, particularly in the savanna and Sahel regions. Although there are several hundred distinct ethnic groups in the region, they can be divided into three main cultural groups. The largest group consists of CULTIVATORS, such as the Mandinka in Senegal and The Gambia, the Yoruba in Nigeria, the Mende in Sierra

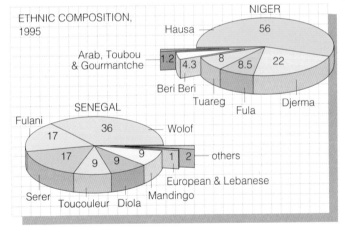

ETHNIC COMPOSITION, 1995

NIGER
Hausa — 56
Arab, Toubou & Gourmantche — 1.2 4.3 8 8.5 22
Beri Beri
Tuareg Fula Djerma

SENEGAL
Fulani — 17 36 — Wolof
17 9 9 9 1 2 — others
Serer Toucouleur Diola Mandingo European & Lebanese

Leone, and the Ashante in Ghana. The two smaller groups are the PASTORALISTS, such as the Fulani in the savanna region and the Tuareg farther north toward the Sahara Desert, and fishing communities, such as the Ewe of Ghana and Togo and the Fanti of Ghana. Urban-based groups are associated with crafts and light industries and include the Yoruba and the famous metalworkers of the ancient Benin Kingdom, located around Benin City in southern Nigeria.

DAILY LIFE

POVERTY

There are some elements of daily life that are common throughout West Africa. Poverty is the overwhelming issue. Four out of the five poorest countries in the world are located in the region, Niger being the poorest. The poverty of the region is highlighted by the fact that Sierra Leone has the world's lowest life expectancy (40 years), and Niger has the world's highest infant mortality rate (nearly 20%). Burkina Faso and Niger have the highest rates of adult illiteracy (over 80%), and the lowest ratio of doctors-to-population in the world. There is only one doctor for every 57,000 people in Burkina Faso.

URBAN LIFE

Not all of West Africa's people are poor. In every city there are wealthy business-people and others with a high standard of living. The gap between rich and poor is large and often clearly visible. In Guinea-Bissau, for example, the wealthiest 20% of the population has nearly 60% of the country's money, whereas the poorest 40% has less than 10%. This means that even in

▲ *These are workers' houses near a manganese mine in Ghana. Townships often spring up close to mines or cash crop fields.*

the cities the great majority of people are very poor, living in overcrowded housing with inadequate facilities and a high risk of disease, illness, and crime. Most of these people are, however, very enterprising and positive in spirit. Many of them work in the INFORMAL SECTOR of the economy, selling papers, shining shoes, washing windshields, working in backstreet industries, or selling produce brought in from the surrounding rural areas.

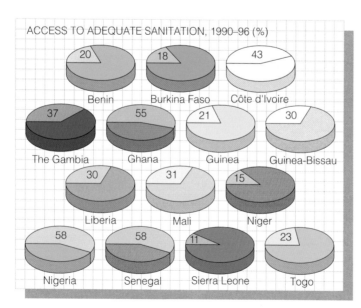

ACCESS TO ADEQUATE SANITATION, 1990–96 (%)

20 Benin	18 Burkina Faso	43 Côte d'Ivoire
37 The Gambia	55 Ghana	21 Guinea · 30 Guinea-Bissau
30 Liberia	31 Mali	15 Niger
58 Nigeria	58 Senegal	11 Sierra Leone · 23 Togo

◀ *Adults and children alike are taught basic health care at a rural workshop in Sierra Leone. Health is generally very poor in West Africa, particularly in rural areas.*

RURAL LIFE

For most people who live in rural areas, daily life revolves around working on the land to earn a living. This may involve large-scale commercial farming, but it is more likely to mean working on the small family farm or herding livestock between water holes and pasture. The milk is offered in exchange for vegetables in rural markets.

The extended family live together in one household, which is responsible for providing food and income for all its members. Households commonly include a mother, a father, grandparents, unmarried relatives, and many children. Under Muslim tradition, men may have up to four wives.

INFANT MORTALITY, 1995 (deaths under 1 year old per 1,000)	
4	Japan
6	U.K.
8	U.S.
86	Burkina Faso
128	Guinea
134	Guinea-Bissau
144	Liberia
164	Sierra Leone
191	Niger

▶ *Soccer is an obsession throughout much of West Africa. Boys, like these in Nigeria, take advantage of any open space to practice their game.*

◀ *In rural West Africa, the traditional walled family compound with a group of thatched huts is still a common feature of the landscape.*

RELIGION AND EDUCATION

Islam is the most widespread religion in West Africa. In Senegal, for example, 92% of the population are Muslim. In Nigeria, the most heavily populated country, about 50% of the population are Muslim. Christianity, introduced by colonial missionaries in the 19th century, is also important, particularly in the south of the region in countries such as Ghana and Nigeria. Many communities,

RELIGIONS (%)

Muslim

Indigenous

Christian

other

NIGERIA 50 40 10

MALI 90 9 1

SIERRA LEONE 60 30 10

SENEGAL 92 6 2

GHANA 30 24 38 8

BENIN 15 15 70

LIBERIA 20 10 70

▶ *There are hundreds of people at Friday afternoon prayers in Ouagadougou, the capital of Burkina Faso. Mosques are a distinctive feature in most West African towns and cities.*

◀ *Children in Mali carrying their desks to school at the start of a new term. Even those lucky enough to go to school may still have to bring their own equipment.*

particularly in rural areas, hold on to their traditional religions and beliefs. The highest proportion of these is found in Benin (around 70%).

Education is regarded as a privilege among West Africans. Although about 70% of the children attend elementary school, the numbers staying on beyond this level are very small. In many Muslim communities, there is a tendency for girls to stay at home

ADULT ILLITERACY, 1995 (%)

63	81	60
Benin	Burkina Faso	Côte d'Ivoire
61	36	64 ... 45
The Gambia	Ghana	Guinea ... Guinea-Bissau
66	69	62
Liberia	Mali	Mauritania
86	43	67 ... 69
Niger	Nigeria	Senegal ... Sierra Leone
48	less than 5	less than 5
Togo	U.K.	U.S.

with their mothers, so levels of female education and literacy are often well below those of males. In Mauritania, for example, where over 90% of people are Muslim, 50% of males are literate compared with only 26% of females.

HOLIDAYS

West Africans celebrate a large number of holidays. Probably the most important are the Muslim holiday of Eid-al-Fitr, which celebrates the end of the month-long fast of Ramadan, and the Christian holidays of Christmas and Easter. Other festivals are associated with the farming calendar, such as the New Yam festival, celebrated by Nigeria's Yoruba people at harvesttime.

KEY FACTS

● Giving and receiving kola nuts is a traditional exchange of friendship. These chestnut-sized nuts with a bitter taste are chewed and have the same effect as caffeine in tea and coffee.

● During 1994 in Guinea-Bissau, 77% of boys and 42% of girls were enrolled in primary school. At secondary level the figures fell to just 9% for boys and 4% for girls.

● In countries like Togo and Benin, items such as televisions are a luxury. In 1993 there were only 6 sets per 1,000 people compared with 60 in Côte d'Ivoire, the highest in the region, or 813 in the U.S.— the highest level in the world.

Before they became independent, the 16 countries of West Africa were colonial territories belonging to three European powers—Great Britain, France, and Portugal. The only exception to this was Liberia, which has been an independent state since 1847. Liberia's origins go back to the American Colonization Society, founded in 1816 to settle black Americans in Africa, from where many ancestors of black Americans had been taken as slaves. Liberia has maintained close links with the U.S. It was founded with an American-style constitution, and the capital city, Monrovia, was named after U.S. President James Monroe. The black settlers became known as "Americo–Liberians" and have very different cultural characteristics from other African cultural groups in Liberia.

In the neighboring country of Sierra Leone, the British similarly moved groups of freed black slaves, known as Creoles, from Caribbean plantations. The city of Freetown is located on the spot where they were settled. Like the Americo–Liberians, the Creoles have a distinct culture compared with other Sierra Leonean peoples.

It was West Africa that led the way to African independence south of the Sahara. The first country to be granted independence was Gold Coast, renamed Ghana in 1957, under the dynamic leadership of Kwame Nkrumah. Many West African countries

▲ *In August 1983 Captain Thomas Sankara, a young army officer, seized power in Burkina Faso with his National Revolutionary Council. He was one of many young military leaders who emerged in West Africa after independence.*

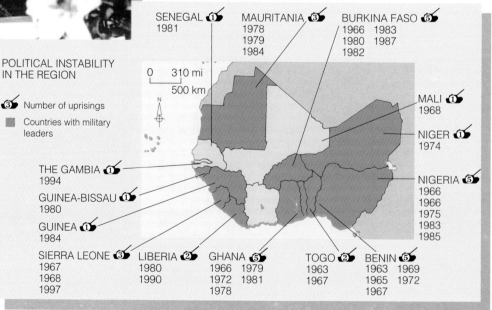

POLITICAL INSTABILITY IN THE REGION

3 Number of uprisings

■ Countries with military leaders

0   310 mi
     500 km

SENEGAL **1**
1981

MAURITANIA **3**
1978
1979
1984

BURKINA FASO **5**
1966 1983
1980 1987
1982

MALI **1**
1968

NIGER **1**
1974

NIGERIA **5**
1966
1966
1975
1983
1985

THE GAMBIA **1**
1994

GUINEA-BISSAU **1**
1980

GUINEA **1**
1984

SIERRA LEONE **3**
1967
1968
1997

LIBERIA **2**
1980
1990

GHANA **5**
1966 1979
1972 1981
1978

TOGO **2**
1963
1967

BENIN **5**
1963 1969
1965 1972
1967

◀ *In 1995 Liberia was beginning to emerge from a decade of turmoil and civil war. Many civilians lost their lives, and children as young as 14 were recruited to fight as soldiers.*

quickly followed Ghana in gaining independence. All the French colonial states were granted independence in 1960 and have retained strong ties with France. The exception was Guinea, which gained its independence in 1958 and severed many of its ties with France. Following Ghana, Great Britain's other West African territories of

KEY FACTS
● Nigeria has the biggest military force in West Africa with 76,500 troops in 1994, compared with just 800 in The Gambia.
● The disruption caused by civil war in Liberia reduced the GROSS NATIONAL PRODUCT (GNP) PER CAPITA from US$699 in 1991 to just US$390 in 1995. Iron ore production fell from 14.2 million tons in 1988 to 1.9 million in 1992.
● Leopold Senghor became Senegal's first president when the country became independent in 1960, but he stepped down from power voluntarily in 1980. Senghor is well known for his poetry and writing on "negritude," in which he considers the significance of being black and celebrates African civilization and values.

INDEPENDENCE

REPUBLIC OF BENIN
formerly **Dahomey**
former colonial power: **France**
Independence: **August 1, 1960**

BURKINA FASO
formerly **Upper Volta**
former colonial power: **France**
Independence: **August 5, 1960**

REPUBLIC OF CAPE VERDE
formerly **Cape Verde Islands**
former colonial power: **Portugal**
Independence: **July 5, 1975**

REPUBLIC OF CÔTE D'IVOIRE
formerly **Côte d'Ivoire**
former colonial power: **France**
Independence: **August 7, 1960**

REPUBLIC OF THE GAMBIA
formerly **Gambia**
former colonial power: **Great Britain**
Independence: **February 18, 1965**

REPUBLIC OF GHANA
formerly **Gold Coast**
former colonial power: **Great Britain**
Independence: **March 6, 1957**

REPUBLIC OF GUINEA
formerly **French Guinea**
former colonial power: **France**
Independence: **October 12, 1958**

REPUBLIC OF GUINEA-BISSAU
formerly **Portuguese Guinea**
former colonial power: **Portugal**
Independence: **September 10, 1974**

REPUBLIC OF LIBERIA
formerly unnamed
former colonial power: **None**
Independence: **July 26, 1847**

REPUBLIC OF MALI
formerly **French Sudan**
former colonial power: **France**
Independence: **September 22, 1960**

ISLAMIC REPUBLIC OF MAURITANIA
formerly **Mauritania**
former colonial power: **France**
Independence: **November 28, 1960**

REPUBLIC OF NIGER
formerly **Niger**
former colonial power: **France**
Independence: **August 3, 1960**

FEDERAL REPUBLIC OF NIGERIA
formerly **Nigeria**
former colonial power: **Great Britain**
Independence: **October 1, 1960**

REPUBLIC OF SENEGAL
formerly **Senegal**
former colonial power: **France**
Independence: **August 20, 1960**

REPUBLIC OF SIERRA LEONE
formerly **Sierra Leone**
former colonial power: **Great Britain**
Independence: **April 24, 1961**

REPUBLIC OF TOGO
formerly **French Togo**
former colonial power: **France/Germany**
Independence: **April 27, 1960**

Nigeria, Sierra Leone, and The Gambia were granted independence in 1960, 1961, and 1965 respectively. The last countries to receive their independence were the two small Portuguese territories of Guinea-Bissau and Cape Verde in 1974 and 1975 respectively.

Upon gaining their independence, a number of West African states seemed to have a bright future. But nearly all have since suffered from some degree of unstable government. Often one government has been overthrown by another or a military regime has replaced a civilian democracy. Some countries have had five or more military coups since gaining their independence,

notably Benin, Burkina Faso, Ghana, and Nigeria. The West African states need to develop strong economies if they are to compete effectively in the world markets, but continuing political unrest can make this hard to achieve. The unstable political situation in Nigeria, for example, has prevented the country from developing what could be one of the strongest economies in Africa. Certain other states, like Ghana, have managed to overcome long periods of instability. Under the leadership of Jerry Rawlings, Ghana has made considerable economic progress during the 1980s and the 1990s.

◄ *Ghana was the first state in West Africa to gain independence. Its popular leader, Kwame Nkrumah, had great visions of a united and independent Africa.*

▼ *Jerry Rawlings, who seized power in Ghana as a military leader, later won a democratic election as a civilian candidate in November 1992, taking 58% of the vote.*

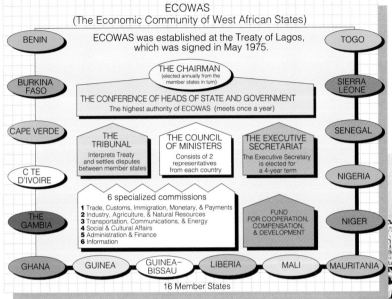

ECOWAS
(The Economic Community of West African States)

ECOWAS was established at the Treaty of Lagos, which was signed in May 1975.

BENIN		TOGO
BURKINA FASO	**THE CHAIRMAN** (elected annually from the member states in turn)	SIERRA LEONE

THE CONFERENCE OF HEADS OF STATE AND GOVERNMENT
The highest authority of ECOWAS (meets once a year)

CAPE VERDE				SENEGAL

	THE TRIBUNAL Interprets Treaty and settles disputes between member states	**THE COUNCIL OF MINISTERS** Consists of 2 representatives from each country	**THE EXECUTIVE SECRETARIAT** The Executive Secretary is elected for a 4-year term	
C TE D'IVOIRE				NIGERIA

6 specialized commissions
1 Trade, Customs, Immigration, Monetary, & Payments
2 Industry, Agriculture, & Natural Resources
3 Transportation, Communications, & Energy
4 Social & Cultural Affairs
5 Administration & Finance
6 Information

FUND FOR COOPERATION, COMPENSATION, & DEVELOPMENT

THE GAMBIA					NIGER
GHANA	GUINEA	GUINEA–BISSAU	LIBERIA	MALI	MAURITANIA

16 Member States

ECOWAS

Nkrumah and other political figures felt that, with so many states in the region and some of them quite small, there was an urgent need for them to cooperate with one another much in the same way as the European Economic Community (EEC). Three years after Nkrumah's death, the Treaty of Lagos was signed (in May 1975) by 15 West African states. This set up the Economic Community of West African States (ECOWAS). Cape Verde became the sixteenth member two years later, in 1977. ECOWAS aims to promote "the rapid and balanced development of West Africa" and remove barriers to trade and commerce in order to create greater unity. The ECOWAS states have established an international military force called ECOMOG (the ECOWAS Monitoring Group). This has

played a key role in resolving several of the region's conflicts. ECOWAS has great potential, but there is some concern in the region that the organization is too heavily dominated by Nigeria.

▶ *Political supporters of the opposition party celebrate the opening of the new parliament in Freetown, Sierra Leone, after democratic elections were held in 1996.*

FOOD AND FARMING

CASH CROPS

Farming is the main activity in West Africa, employing over 70% of the population. The region is an important producer of cocoa, coffee, peanuts, and cotton. West Africa produces over half the world's cocoa beans, and Côte d'Ivoire is the world's largest producing country. Côte d'Ivoire is also the world's ninth largest producer of coffee, and Nigeria and Senegal are the fourth and sixth largest producers of peanuts. Other important exported commodities include cotton from Mali, Côte d'Ivoire, and Nigeria.

These crops are known as cash crops, which means they are mainly grown for sale in the world markets rather than for consumption by local people. Cash crops are normally worth more money than local crops, but there is always a risk that prices will fall due to changing world demands. Price changes can greatly affect West

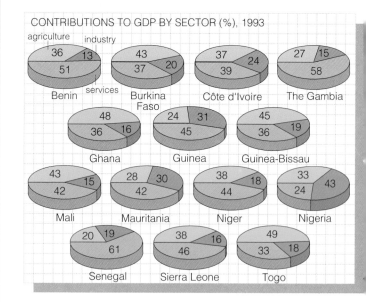

▲ *Intensive vegetable cultivation is becoming increasingly common in West Africa, particularly beside large rivers such as the Niger. The vegetables are sold in urban markets or exported.*

CONTRIBUTIONS TO GDP BY SECTOR (%), 1993

	agriculture	industry	services
Benin	36	13	51
Burkina Faso	43	20	37
Côte d'Ivoire	37	24	39
The Gambia	27	15	58
Ghana	48	16	36
Guinea	24	31	45
Guinea-Bissau	45	19	36
Mali	43	15	42
Mauritania	28	30	42
Niger	38	18	44
Nigeria	33	43	24
Senegal	20	19	61
Sierra Leone	38	16	46
Togo	49	18	33

KEY FACTS

● Much of Cape Verde is dry and barren, so large quantities of food are imported. The country's fishing industry, however, employs over 3,000 people and provides valuable export earnings.

● Nigeria, Côte d'Ivoire, Benin, Ghana, and Togo are the world's top five producers of yams. In 1993 they produced 27,766,200 tons or 89.7% of world production.

● In the pastoral countries of West Africa, livestock are more important than crops. In 1993 Mali had over 5.5 million cattle, and Mauritania had nearly 1 million camels.

● In 1992 none of the West African states used more than 18 pounds of fertilizer per acre of agricultural land. This compares with 97 pounds in the United States.

▼ Women with head-loaded beans walk past an irrigation gantry watering a field of sugarcane. Because of the seasonal shortages of water, large-scale irrigation is vital to commercial agriculture in West Africa.

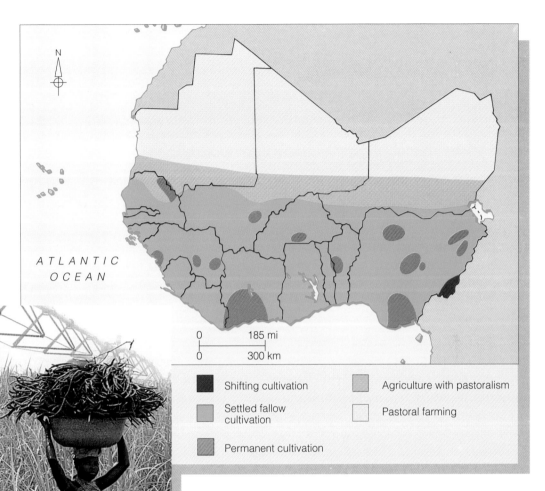

ATLANTIC OCEAN

| 0 | 185 mi |
| 0 | 300 km |

- ■ Shifting cultivation
- ▨ Settled fallow cultivation
- ▨ Permanent cultivation
- ▨ Agriculture with pastoralism
- ☐ Pastoral farming

SUBSISTENCE FARMING

Although agricultural produce makes a valuable contribution to a country's economy, the main aim of most West African farmers is to feed their families. A wide range of food crops are grown. The choice of crops varies greatly throughout the region, depending on soil, rainfall, and temperature conditions. African farmers are very skilled and understand their local

African producers. Many farmers try to grow a range of different crops so that if the price of one crop falls, they still have others to sell. Another reason for growing several crops is to guard against the risk of drought, disease, or pests, all of which can ruin one crop but leave others untouched.

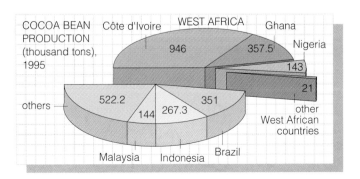

COCOA BEAN PRODUCTION (thousand tons), 1995

WEST AFRICA

Côte d'Ivoire 946
Ghana 357.5
Nigeria 143
21 other West African countries
others 522.2
Malaysia 144
Indonesia 267.3
Brazil 351

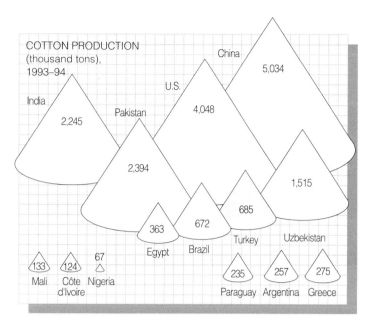

COTTON PRODUCTION
(thousand tons),
1993–94

China 5,034
U.S. 4,048
Pakistan 2,394
India 2,245
Uzbekistan 1,515
Turkey 685
Brazil 672
Egypt 363
Greece 275
Argentina 257
Paraguay 235
Mali 133
Côte d'Ivoire 124
Nigeria 67

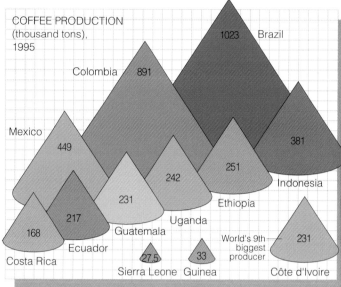

COFFEE PRODUCTION
(thousand tons),
1995

Brazil 1023
Colombia 891
Mexico 449
Indonesia 381
Ethiopia 251
Uganda 242
Guatemala 231
Côte d'Ivoire 231 — World's 9th biggest producer
Ecuador 217
Costa Rica 168
Guinea 33
Sierra Leone 27.5

environment at least as well as the best-trained scientists. In many cases their knowledge is much greater. By growing crops with different water needs, such as cassava (which requires very little water compared with corn), farmers can ensure that they will have some food even if the amount of rainfall is relatively low.

Most farmers grow staple crops. These are crops that form the basis of the household diet, like wheat and potatoes in the U.K. and U.S., or rice in much of Asia. West Africa's key staple crops are cassava, corn, millet, rice, sorghum (guinea corn), and yams. In addition to these, farmers also grow vegetables such as sweet potatoes, chilies, tomatoes, and beans, and various fruits, including mangoes, bananas, and papaws. Farmers commonly plant a number of crops in the same field—a practice known as "intercropping." Apart from providing a more varied diet, the high density of crop cover also protects the soil from erosion during heavy storms. At first sight many fields look

◀ *Fulani children patiently wait their turn to collect water from a rural water pump. It is usually the young girls who collect water for the home.*

◀ *Fish are a vital
source of protein
in the diets of
many West African
people. A catch of
fish in Ghana
is sorted into
different varieties
before it is sold in
the market.*

very disorganized, but experts now agree
that this method is, in fact, a good way of
adapting to environmental conditions.

West Africans also eat meat from
chickens, sheep, and goats, and use milk
from cattle. Cattle are very important to
African farmers, and to many pastoral groups
they are a symbol of wealth. The Fulani
people, who range across the savanna and
Sahel regions of West Africa, are the main
pastoral group. Today relatively few Fulani
are entirely NOMADIC. Most have fixed
settlements around which they grow their
crops. However they still retain a strong
attachment to their livestock and are renowned
for their expertise. Milk, yogurt, and butter are
sold by Fulani women and can command high
prices in urban markets.

FISHING

As a result of the long Atlantic coastline of
West Africa, many people engage in fishing.
The Fanti and Ewe people of southern Ghana
are well known for their skills as fishermen.
The vast wetlands of Mali's inland Niger Delta
and the Hadejia-Nguru region of northeastern
Nigeria also provide valuable fishing grounds,
as do artificial lakes such as Lake Volta in
Ghana and Lake Kainji in Nigeria. In the
inland Niger Delta, the Bozo and Somono
people are important fishing communities.

KEY FACTS

● Completed in 1976, the Tiga Dam, south
of Kano in northern Nigeria, irrigates over
148,260 acres (60,000 hectares) of land on
the Kano River Project, where crops such as
wheat, rice, and tomatoes are grown.
● Fanti fishermen from Ghana have
migrated westward along the coast and
settled in The Gambia. From a settlement
called Ghana Town, they fish in the Atlantic
Ocean for shark and ray, which are then
dried, salted, and bagged before being sent
home to Ghana.
● Ghana and Senegal are the main fishing
countries in West Africa. In 1992 they
landed 469,700 tons and 359,700 tons
respectively. This is important in the region
but insignificant when compared with the
U.S. catch of 6,160,000 tons.

◄ *Here women are harvesting rice in The Gambia. It is estimated that women produce more than 70% of Africa's food.*

RURAL DEVELOPMENT

Many people have attempted to increase agricultural production and improve the living standards of rural people in West Africa. However, many development plans have not succeeded because outsiders have not understood farming practices and the needs of local people. In The Gambia, for example, attempts to improve the production of swamp rice failed because it was assumed that rice farmers were men.

In fact, rice in The Gambia is regarded by the Mandinka and Wolof people as a "woman's crop." It is the women who have a wealth of knowledge about its production and processing. The construction of dams, reservoirs, and irrigation projects in semiarid

▼ *With support from development agencies, in this case in Niger, women are very successful in producing staple foods such as millet and corn.*

regions, such as northern Nigeria, has benefited some people but caused problems for others. Poor farmers have often been unable to buy land. Fulani pastoralists have lost valuable grazing areas, and their migratory routes have been disrupted. These dams have changed the flow of the river, so that there is now no annual flood and fewer fish to be caught.

Some development projects, however, have been more successful, particularly where developers have worked closely with local people. In northwest Burkina Faso, the Mossi people have for years been laying lines of stones across their fields to prevent erosion. The main problem they faced was a shortage of stones, so a development agency has now provided a truck to transport stones to the Mossi villages. Women's groups in The Gambia have been given seeds and tools to grow vegetables during the long dry season. Wells have been sunk, and in some cases pumps driven by solar

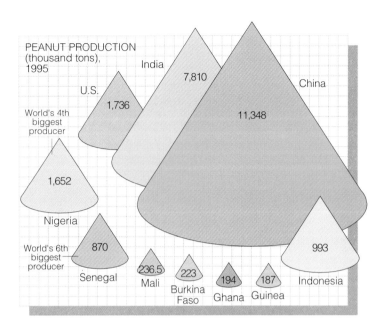

PEANUT PRODUCTION (thousand tons), 1995

- India 7,810
- U.S. 1,736
- China 11,348
- Nigeria — World's 4th biggest producer 1,652
- Senegal — World's 6th biggest producer 870
- Mali 236.5
- Burkina Faso 223
- Ghana 194
- Guinea 187
- Indonesia 993

power have been installed to raise water on to the fields. The introduction of refrigerated trucks in the future could make it possible for vegetables to be transported long distances to the tourist hotels on the Atlantic coast, where demand is high.

► **Peppers for sale in a market at Onitsha, in southern Nigeria. Large food surpluses can be produced if the rains are plentiful. This is reflected in the many colorful markets throughout West Africa.**

TRADE AND INDUSTRY

Most West African countries continue to trade mainly with their former colonial power. For example, 30% of Senegalese exports go to France, and 37.8% of its imports come from France. Similarly, Ghana's main trading links are with the U.K., with 13.8% of exports and 16% of imports. Despite ECOWAS' attempts to promote trade within the region, relatively few goods are exchanged between West African countries.

Large quantities of minerals (bauxite, iron ore, uranium, diamonds) and agricultural commodities (coffee, cocoa, cotton, peanuts) are exported in a raw, unprocessed state.

Processing is then mainly undertaken in European countries where, as a result, the value of the commodity is considerably increased. West African producers and producing countries usually receive only

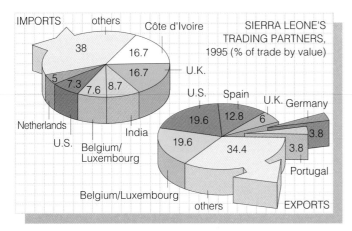

SIERRA LEONE'S TRADING PARTNERS, 1995 (% of trade by value)

IMPORTS: others 38, Côte d'Ivoire 16.7, U.K. 16.7, U.S. 8.7, India 7.6, Belgium/Luxembourg 7.3, Netherlands 5

EXPORTS: Spain 19.6, U.S. 19.6, Belgium/Luxembourg 34.4, U.K. 12.8, Germany 6, Portugal 3.8, others 3.8

KEY FACTS

● Tourism contributes over 12% of The Gambia's Gross National Product (GNP) and employs more than 35,000 people. The government is encouraging further expansion by giving free land to build hotels on the coast. A new airport terminal was completed in 1997.

● Many of the poorer West African states rely heavily on official development assistance (aid) from wealthier countries and international banks. In 1994 70% of Guinea-Bissau's GNP resulted from aid money.

● Several countries in West Africa rely heavily on a single product. Niger relied on uranium for 65% of its export earnings in 1991, a 5% fall since 1978 due mainly to falling world prices.

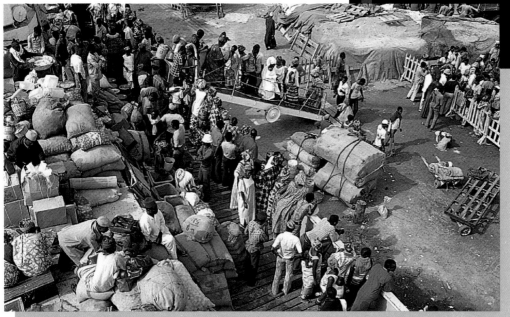

◀ *Ports are the major focus for trade between West African countries and those farther away. Dakar, in Senegal, is one of the region's major ports. When a new boat arrives, it becomes the center of great activity.*

◀ *A factory making plywood at Burutu, in southern Nigeria. Most of West Africa's agricultural products and minerals are exported in a raw state, but countries can benefit considerably if they process raw materials locally.*

a small proportion of the value of the end product.

Bottling plants for the soft drinks industry, where brands such as Coca-Cola are produced under local licenses, are the most visible industries in many West African towns and cities. Food processing is also important. In Senegal this accounts for almost half of all industrial production and includes flour mills, a peanut oil mill, a fish cannery, and a sugar refinery. Heavy industry is restricted to a few key centers such as aluminum smelting in Ghana and Guinea, and car assembly and petroleum refining in Nigeria.

Tourism is not as well developed in West Africa as it is in other parts of Africa. Although the region has tremendous potential, with its natural beauty, tropical sandy beaches, and fascinating cultural heritage, only relatively few areas have the necessary tourist hotels and INFRASTRUCTURE. An exception is The Gambia, which has invested heavily in package-tourism development, even though it has only a 40-mile (64-km) coastline. Ghana and the Casamance region of southern Senegal are also increasingly popular tourist destinations, but most other parts of West Africa are visited mainly by individual travelers.

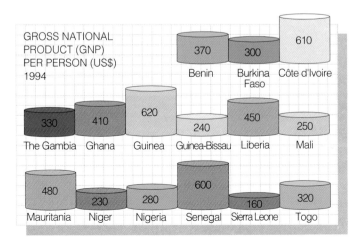

GROSS NATIONAL PRODUCT (GNP) PER PERSON (US$) 1994

			Benin 370	Burkina Faso 300	Côte d'Ivoire 610
The Gambia 330	Ghana 410	Guinea 620	Guinea-Bissau 240	Liberia 450	Mali 250
Mauritania 480	Niger 230	Nigeria 280	Senegal 600	Sierra Leone 160	Togo 320

TRANSPORTATION

est Africa's transportation system is poorly developed compared with those of Europe or North America. Although paved roads connect the main centers, many are in poor condition and badly potholed, making travel in the rainy season particularly difficult. Few people own cars, so most use public buses or minibuses known variously as "mammy wagons" in Nigeria and "poda podas" in Sierra Leone. Road travel can be dangerous, with busy roads and poorly maintained and overcrowded vehicles, leading to fatal accidents.

Unlike eastern and southern Africa, railroads are not well developed in West Africa. Railroad routes were mainly constructed during the colonial period and tend to consist of single lines connecting coastal ports with important mines and cash-crop areas. There are no railroad links between French- and English-speaking countries. Only Nigeria has anything resembling a rail "network," although in the mid-1990s only a few trains were operating because of lack of maintenance.

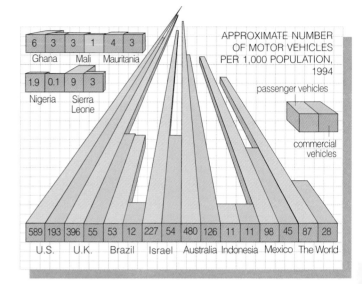

APPROXIMATE NUMBER OF MOTOR VEHICLES PER 1,000 POPULATION, 1994

passenger vehicles

commercial vehicles

Ghana		Mali		Mauritania	
6	3	3	1	4	3

Nigeria		Sierra Leone	
1.9	0.1	9	3

U.S.		U.K.		Brazil		Israel		Australia		Indonesia		Mexico		The World	
589	193	396	55	53	12	227	54	480	126	11	11	98	45	87	28

▲ *Unpaved roads can easily become impassable during the rainy season. Trucks often get bogged down for days at a time.*

◀ *A donkey cart is a prized possession for many poor rural families. People and goods can be carried to and from the fields and market.*

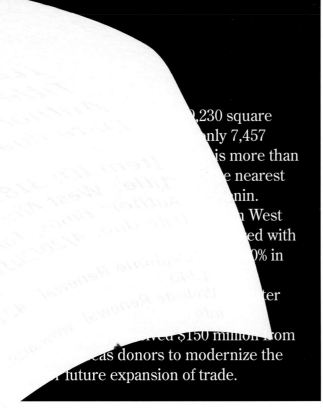

,230 square
nly 7,457
is more than
e nearest
nin.
West
ed with
0% in

ter

d $150 million from
as donors to modernize the
future expansion of trade.

There are also relatively few airline connections between former French and British colonies, but there are well-developed links with European cities such as Paris and London. Air transportation could be the best way of covering the long distances between the region's major cities, but the development of air travel has been limited by the high

cost of running a national airline and by the fact that many people cannot afford the fares.

Lagos, Abidjan, Dakar, and Freetown are important West African seaports, vital for importing and exporting bulky goods. Some new ports have been created, such as Tema in Ghana. Before the 1950s, Tema was a small fishing village, but now it has a large artificial harbor constructed to serve the Akosombo Dam and Accra, the country's capital.

For most West Africans, who cannot afford to use expensive modern means of transportation, the main forms of travel are by bicycle, donkey cart, or on foot. Village blacksmiths can easily make simple donkey carts out of recycled metal from disused vehicles.

▼ *For centuries, goods have been transported along the Niger River in Mali in traditional boats known as "pirogues."*

THE ENVIRONMENT

West Africa has a number of bustling cities, but it also has vast, relatively undeveloped areas. One major difference from eastern and southern Africa is that the West African region has very few large mammals. Village elders, however, can remember when elephants, lions, and other animals roamed the forest and savanna. Sadly, most have been killed by hunters or displaced by expanding human settlements. Today West Africa is famous for its bird life. Each year a large number of ornithologists (experts on bird life) visit countries such as The Gambia to study both resident and migrant birds.

West Africa's rapidly growing population has put great pressure on the environment. The main environmental problems are water shortages, pollution, deforestation, soil erosion, and desertification. These problems

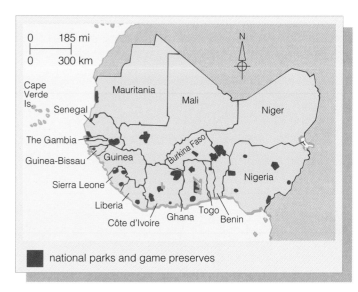

national parks and game preserves

are often closely related. For example, the clearance of tree cover for cultivation exposes the soil to a higher risk of erosion. Heavy rains may wash away nutrient-rich topsoils, reduce fertility, and lead to falling crop yields. Some people have suggested

◀ *Abuko Nature Reserve in The Gambia has been a long-standing example of how West Africa can preserve its remaining wildlife. The park is enclosed to protect it from encroaching settlements and farming.*

► *The African darter is one of a wide variety of birds native to West Africa that can be seen in many of the region's national parks. Visitors also come to see the many birds that migrate to West Africa to escape the European winter.*

that these processes, over a prolonged period, may eventually lead to desertification. After one or two good rainy seasons, however, the growth of natural vegetation will sometimes restore fertility and reduce the threat of erosion.

In towns the main environmental problems are related to overcrowding and poor urban planning. Housing is often badly built and located haphazardly on any available land. Shortages of clean water and inadequate sanitation facilities are major problems, especially in overcrowded city slums. People are sometimes forced to drink water that may have been used for washing, cleaning clothes, and watering livestock. The region's major diseases, such as hepatitis, typhoid, dysentery, and diarrhea are transmitted through using dirty water. Malaria is often transmitted by mosquitoes, which breed near stagnant or slow-moving water. Infection rates are often very high in crowded slum areas. Many rural areas also lack safe water and sanitation facilities, and people will use the nearest stream, river, or lake for drinking water and washing.

Mineral exploitation can have a significant impact on the environment.

ACCESS TO SAFE WATER, 1990–96 (%)

Country	%
Benin	50
Burkina Faso	78
Côte d'Ivoire	75
The Gambia	48
Ghana	65
Guinea	55
Guinea-Bissau	59
Liberia	46
Mali	45
Mauritania	66
Niger	54
Nigeria	51
Senegal	52
Sierra Leone	34
Togo	63
China	67
Brazil	73
India	81
Japan	97
Vietnam	43

► **Trash builds up around a market in Benin. The rapid growth of the cities means that services such as trash disposal are often inadequate.**

◄ **On the outskirts of Freetown, Sierra Leone, local farmers have reclaimed land from the mangrove swamps. The local environment has been transformed, and food is produced for both domestic consumption and for sale.**

◀ *The Niger Delta, in Nigeria, has rich oil reserves, but extraction can lead to severe environmental damage to the fragile wetlands.*

action, such as the Naam movement founded, in 1967, in Yatenga Province, Burkina Faso. In this region with poor soils and frequent droughts, the Naam movement encourages local communities to work together in projects such as establishing fruit tree nurseries, planting trees to supply fuel, and building dams to irrigate rice, vegetables, and fruit trees.

Open-cast tin mining on the Jos Plateau in Nigeria and diamond mining in Sierra Leone have led to widespread devastation of farmland. In the Niger Delta of Nigeria, major international concern, as well as complaints from local communities, have focused on pollution caused by drilling for oil. Farmers' crops have been ruined, and intense gas flares burn constantly, close to villages. West African governments have started to recognize the importance of protecting their natural environments for future generations. They have set up several national parks to save both animals and their habitats from further destruction.

Local people are often more anxious to conserve the environment, since many of them directly depend on it for their survival. There are many examples of local community

KEY FACTS

● In 15 years, Burkina Faso has lost nearly 60% of its trees through drought, over-grazing, bushfires, and uncontrolled felling. The water table has fallen by about 65 feet (20 m) in the last two decades.
● Between 1980 and 1989, Côte d'Ivoire cleared its forests at an average of 1,260,200 acres (510,000 ha) per year or 5.2% of total reserves—one of the fastest rates in the world.
● Throughout West Africa, in 1996, only about 54% of the population had access to safe water and about 31% had adequate sanitation facilities.
● Small-scale illegal operations by local prospectors can cause serious environmental damage. In May 1992, about 100 people were killed when an illegally dug diamond mine in Sierra Leone caved in.
● In 1997 Côte d'Ivoire decided to ban the ivory trade in order to limit the threats to its remaining elephant population of about 2,000. Côte d'Ivoire has the largest elephant population in West Africa after Nigeria.

THE FUTURE

◀ *Nigeria has spent millions of dollars in building the new capital city of Abuja, located in the sparsely settled "middle belt" of the country. Government ministries and foreign embassies are gradually moving into the new city.*

West Africa is probably the poorest region in the world, with the lowest life expectancy and highest infant mortality rates. The region and its people have a long way to go to catch up with their fellow Africans, let alone reach the standards of living enjoyed by the majority of people in North America or Western Europe. Some of the major developmental priorities for the future include ensuring clean water supplies, basic health care, and primary education. Transportation, electricity, and sanitation also need to be improved. As the population grows rapidly, particularly in the towns and cities, adequate food supplies and the provision of low-cost, high-density housing becomes a vital priority. It also is important that the rural areas not be neglected, since this is where most people live. If conditions are improved in the countryside, fewer people will feel compelled to migrate to the cities.

KEY FACTS

● With the exception of Guinea-Bissau, all of the West African countries are expected to double their population by the year 2020 if 1993 population growth rates continue.

● HIV is becoming a major threat to many of West Africa's people. In Ghana, by the year 2000, it is estimated that there will be over 150,000 orphans as a result of parents dying from AIDS.

● In 1997 scientists from America and Ghana signed a five-year agreement in Accra to research a treatment for malaria, one of the region's major diseases.

● At a seminar on West Africa's natural resources, held in 1997, it was stated that West Africa's known reserves of oil and gas are so large that there is great scope for expansion if modern methods of extraction are used.

Little progress is likely to be made, however, unless the region is politically and economically stable. Long-term planning has often been interrupted by sudden changes of government. The West African people are, however, enterprising and resourceful and have a positive outlook on life. ECOWAS could point the way to future prosperity and a new spirit of cooperation between the West African states and their peoples. In late 1996 the Ghanaian Kofi Annan, who worked for 30 years at the United Nations (UN), was elected Secretary-General of the UN by the General Assembly in New York. Since a West African now occupies one of the most influential positions in the world, this may help to focus greater attention on the region in the future.

▲ *These are students at the University of Benin, in Nigeria. Education is highly valued in West Africa. Many parts of the system, however, such as primary education, are still desperately short of resources.*

FURTHER INFORMATION

● COTE D'IVOIRE TOURISM OFFICE
2424 Massachusetts Avenue NW
Washington, D.C. 20008
● EMBASSY OF GHANA
3512 International Drive NW
Washington, D.C. 20008
● EMBASSY OF LIBERIA
5201 16th Street NW
Washington, D.C. 20011
● EMBASSY OF MALI
2130 R Street NW
Washington, D.C. 20008
● EMBASSY OF MAURITANIA
2129 Leroy Place NW
Washington, D.C. 20008
● EMBASSY OF NIGERIA
1333 16th Street NW
Washington, D.C. 20003

● EMBASSY OF THE REPUBLIC OF SENEGAL
2112 Wyoming Avenue NW
Washington, D.C. 20008

BOOKS ABOUT WEST AFRICA
● *Cote D'Ivoire (Ivory Coast) in Pictures.* Lerner, 1989.
● Hintz, Martin. *Ghana.* Children's Press, 1994.
● Koslow, Philip. *Mali: Crossroads of Africa.* Chelsea House, 1995.
● Owhanda, John. *Nigeria: A Nation of Many Peoples.* Dillon/Silver Burdett, 1997.
● Regan, Colm and Pedar Cremin. *Africa.* Raintree Steck-Vaughn, 1996.
● Wilkins, Frances. *Gambia.* Chelsea House, 1988.

GLOSSARY

ARID
A word used to describe an extremely dry area.

CASH CROPS
Crops that are grown mainly for sale in overseas markets but can also be sold in local markets.

COLONIALISM
A system under which one country occupies and rules another.

CULTIVATORS
People who grow crops to sell and to support themselves and their families.

DELTA
A flat, fan-shaped geographical area where a river splits into many channels. It usually empties into an ocean or sea.

DESERTIFICATION
The process through which a piece of land becomes barren and infertile. It can be caused by drought, deforestation, overcultivation, and soil erosion. It is very difficult to reverse.

GROSS NATIONAL PRODUCT (GNP) PER CAPITA
The total value of all goods and services produced by a country in a year.

HYDROELECTRICITY
Electricity produced by flowing water that drives a generator.

INDEPENDENCE
The transfer of power from a colonial government to a government set up by local people, who are then able to control their own affairs.

INFORMAL SECTOR
The section of the economy that involves the selling of goods or offering of services, sometimes in the streets or in markets. It often is not officially recognized.

INFRASTRUCTURE
A network for transmitting and/or transporting basic things such as water, electricity, information, or vehicles.

LAGOON
A shallow area of water separated from the sea, usually by a sandbar.

LANDLOCKED
A country, territory, or area that has no coastline. Landlocked countries are highly dependent on their neighbors to reach coastal ports, which are important for trade and industry.

NOMADIC
A word describing a wandering lifestyle. It is usually associated with livestock herders moving with their animals in search of pasture and water.

PASTORALISTS (PASTORAL GROUPS)
People who look after animals, sometimes moving long distances in search of water and grazing land.

POLITICAL INSTABILITY
A situation where governments change rapidly, sometimes after political power has been seized by force in a "coup d'état."

RURAL-URBAN MIGRATION
The movement of people from rural areas to towns and cities, often in search of employment.

SAVANNA
A tropical vegetation area consisting of grasses, shrubs, and scattered trees. It is typically dry for most of the year but bursts into life when the first rains arrive.

INDEX